LIFE STORIES / BIOGRAFÍAS

BENJAMÍN FRANKLIN

Gillian Gosman

Traducción al español: Eduardo Alamán

PowerKiDS press™

New York

Published in 2011 by The Rosen Publishing Group, Inc.
29 East 21st Street, New York, NY 10010

First Edition

Editor: Jennifer Way   Spanish translation: Eduardo Alamán
Book Design: Ashley Burrell and Erica Clendening

Photo Credits: Cover (background, inset), p. 11 iStockphoto/Thinkstock; pp. 4–5, 18 SuperStock/Getty Images; p. 6 Kean Collection/Getty Images; pp. 6–7 Apic/Getty Images; pp. 8–9 FPG/Taxi/Getty Images; pp. 9, 12–13, 17 Hulton Archive/Getty Images; pp. 10, 14 MPI/Getty Images; pp. 13 (inset), 16, 22 (top) Fotosearch/Getty Images; pp. 14–15 Library of Congress; pp. 19, 22 (bottom) Buyenlarge/Getty Images; pp. 20–21 Joseph-Siffred Duplessis/The Bridgeman Art Library/Getty Images.

Library of Congress Cataloging-in-Publication Data
Gosman, Gillian.
  [Benjamin Franklin. Spanish & English]
  Benjamín Franklin / by Gillian Gosman. — 1st ed.
      p. cm. — (Life stories = Biografías)
  Includes bibliographical references and index.
  ISBN 978-1-4488-3219-4 (library binding)
  1. Franklin, Benjamin, 1706-1790—Juvenile literature. 2. Statesmen—United States—Biography—Juvenile literature. 3. Scientists—United States—Biography—Juvenile literature. 4. Inventors—United States—Biography—Juvenile literature. 5. Printers—United States—Biography—Juvenile literature. I. Title.
  E302.6.F8G67718 2011
  973.3092—dc22
  [B]
                                    2010036801

Web Sites: Due to the changing nature of Internet links, PowerKids Press has developed an online list of Web sites related to the subject of this book. This site is updated regularly. Please use this link to access the list:
www.powerkidslinks.com/life/franklin/

Manufactured in the United States of America
CPSIA Compliance Information: Batch #WW11PK: For Further Information contact Rosen Publishing, New York, New York at 1-800-237-9932

CONTENTS

CONTENIDO

Meet Benjamin Franklin

Today most cities have services such as a fire department, a library, and a hospital. The idea for each of these services came from or was greatly helped along by Benjamin Franklin.

Franklin believed that a community should have services for the common good. This belief became a key principle in the formation of the United States.

Benjamin Franklin lived a long and interesting life. Many of his ideas played an important part in the formation of the United States.

Conoce a Benjamín Franklin

La mayoría de las ciudades en la actualidad cuentan con servicios tales como un departamento de bomberos, una biblioteca y un hospital. La idea de contar con estos servicios comenzó o fue apoyada en gran medida por Benjamín Franklin.

Franklin creía que una comunidad debía tener servicios para el bien común. Esta forma de pensar se convirtió en un principio clave en la formación de los Estados Unidos.

Benjamin Franklin vivió una vida larga e interesante. Muchas de sus ideas desempeñaron un papel importante en la formación de los Estados Unidos.

Young Ben

Benjamin Franklin was born on January 17, 1706, in Boston, Massachusetts. His father, Josiah, was a candle and soap maker. His mother, Abiah, ran the household, which included 14 other children!

Throughout his life, Franklin was a writer and an inventor. When he was 12, young Benjamin began an **apprenticeship** under his brother James, a printer. Benjamin even started writing, publishing letters under the fake name Silence Dogood.

This picture shows Benjamin starting his apprenticeship at his brother James's print shop.

Esta foto muestra a Franklin durante su aprendizaje en la imprenta de su hermano James.

Here is Franklin as an adult in the lab at his home in Philadelphia. Franklin worked on his inventions in his lab.

Aquí vemos a Franklin de adulto en el laboratorio en su casa de Filadelfia. Franklin trabajó en sus inventos en este laboratorio.

LOS PRIMEROS AÑOS

Benjamín Franklin nació el 17 de enero de 1706, en Boston, Massachusetts. Su padre, Josiah, era fabricante de velas y jabón. Su madre, Abiah, era ama de casa, ¡en un hogar que incluía a 14 niños!

Franklin fue escritor e inventor. Cuando tenía 12 años, el joven Benjamín comenzó un **aprendizaje** en la imprenta de su hermano James. Benjamín comenzó a escribir y a publicar cartas bajo el nombre falso de Silence Dogood.

7

Life in Colonial America

Benjamin Franklin's America was a group of 13 **colonies** ruled by Great Britain. In the middle of the 1700s, the American colonists were getting tired of being ruled by Great Britain.

Great Britain was forcing the colonists to follow laws and pay taxes that did not seem fair to the colonists. Great Britain also decided who would be in charge of the Colonial governments and how court trials would be run.

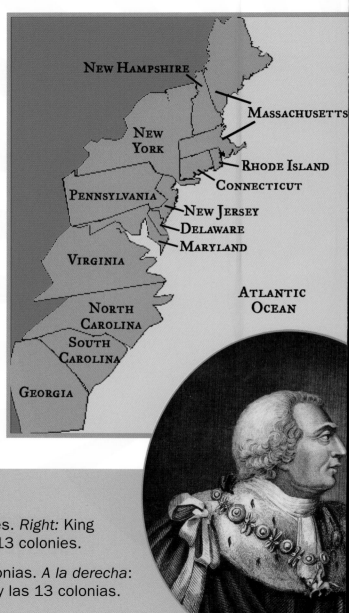

Above: This map shows the 13 colonies. *Right:* King George III ruled Great Britain and the 13 colonies.

Arriba: Este mapa muestra las 13 colonias. *A la derecha:* el Rey Jorge III gobernó Gran Bretaña y las 13 colonias.

This cartoon shows angry colonists speaking out against taxes that they had to pay to Great Britain.

Esta caricatura muestra a colonos enojados hablando en contra de los impuestos que tenían que pagar a Gran Bretaña.

VIDA DURANTE LA COLONIA

En la época de Benjamín Franklin, América era un grupo de 13 **colonias** gobernadas por la Gran Bretaña. A mediados de siglo, en los años 1700, los colonos americanos estaban cansados de ser gobernados por la Gran Bretaña.

La Gran Bretaña los obligaba a seguir sus leyes y pagar impuestos. A los colonos los impuestos no les parecían justos. Además, la Gran Bretaña decidió que se haría cargo de los gobiernos coloniales y de los procesos judiciales.

9

Making His Way

In 1723, Benjamin Franklin left his apprenticeship with his brother in Boston. He wanted to make his way on his own. He ran away to Philadelphia, Pennsylvania. Philadelphia became Franklin's new hometown.

In 1726, Franklin began a self-improvement plan. He took notes on his self-improvement. In 1730, Franklin married Deborah Read. They would raise three children together.

This is Independence Hall, in Philadelphia. Franklin would later be part of the group that met there to write the Declaration of Independence.

Éste es el Independence Hall, en Filadelfia. Franklin formaría parte del grupo que se reunió allí para escribir la Declaración de la Independencia.

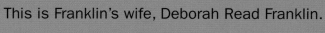

This is Franklin's wife, Deborah Read Franklin.

Ésta es Deborah Read Franklin, esposa de Benjamín Franklin.

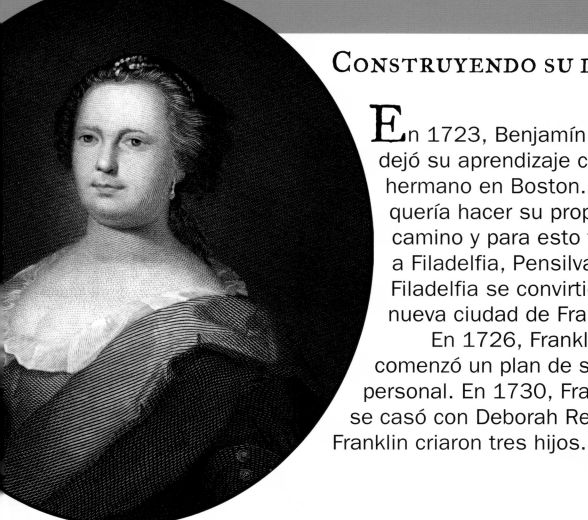

CONSTRUYENDO SU DESTINO

En 1723, Benjamín Franklin dejó su aprendizaje con su hermano en Boston. Franklin quería hacer su propio camino y para esto fue a Filadelfia, Pensilvania. Filadelfia se convirtió en la nueva ciudad de Franklin. En 1726, Franklin comenzó un plan de superación personal. En 1730, Franklin se casó con Deborah Read. Los Franklin criaron tres hijos.

SUPER CITIZEN!

Benjamin Franklin took being a **citizen** seriously. He wanted to make Philadelphia a better place.

In 1732, Franklin began printing *Poor Richard's Almanack*. This magazine was known for its funny sayings. He also formed one of the first fire-fighting companies in America and the Pennsylvania Hospital.

Here Franklin is flying a kite during a thunderstorm to learn about lightning and electricity.

Aquí vemos a Franklin volando una cometa durante una tormenta para aprender sobre electricidad.

¡Un gran ciudadano!

Benjamín Franklin tomó su trabajo como **ciudadano** muy en serio. Franklin quería hacer de Filadelfia un mejor lugar.

En 1732, Franklin comenzó a imprimir una revista llamada *Poor Richard's Almanack*. La revista es conocida por sus divertidas frases. Además, Franklin formó una de las primeras empresas en la lucha contra incendios en los Estados Unidos y el Hospital de Pensilvania.

This is the *Poor Richard's Almanack* from 1744.

Ésta es una edición del *Poor Richard's Almanack* de 1744.

A Public Life

Franklin was active in both city and Colonial government. In 1753, he was given the job of deputy postmaster for all the colonies.

Franklin also spoke out about the colonies' part in the **French and Indian War**. He spoke out about Great Britain's treatment of the colonies, too. In 1757, he was picked to be the Pennsylvania Colony's agent, or representative, in London. He held the job until the 1770s.

This painting shows a battle of the French and Indian War. The war lasted from 1754 until 1763.

Esta pintura muestra una batalla de la Guerra Franco-india. La guerra duró de 1754 a 1763.

OIN, or DIE.

VIDA PÚBLICA

Franklin participó tanto en la ciudad como en el gobierno colonial. En 1753, se le nombró administrador de correo de las colonias.

Además, Franklin habló sobre el papel de las colonias en la **Guerra Franco-india**, y de la forma en que la Gran Bretaña trataba a las colonias. En 1757, fue elegido representante de la colonia de Pensilvania, en Londres. Franklin ocupó este cargo hasta la década de 1770.

America at War

By the 1770s, the American colonists were unhappy with British rule. Living in London, Franklin worked to defend Colonial interests. Great Britain would not change the way it governed the colonies. The colonists were ready for war.

The **American Revolution** began in 1775. Franklin returned to Philadelphia and became Pennsylvania's representative in the **Continental Congress**. This governmental body led the colonies to **independence**.

The American Revolution began on April 19, 1775, with the Battle of Lexington and Concord, shown here.

La Guerra de Independencia comenzó el 19 de abril de 1775, con la batalla de Lexington y Concord, que se muestra aquí.

Franklin returned to Philadelphia from London soon after the American Revolution started.

Poco después de comenzada la Guerra de Independencia, Franklin regresó a Filadelfia desde Londres.

UNA NACIÓN EN GUERRA

En la década de 1770, los colonos americanos estaban descontentos con el dominio británico. En Londres, Franklin trabajó para defender los intereses de las colonias. Pero la Gran Bretaña no iba a cambiar la forma en que regía sus colonias. Los colonos estaban listos para la guerra.

La **Guerra de Independencia** comenzó en 1775. Franklin volvió a Filadelfia y se convirtió en representante de Pensilvania en el **Congreso Continental**. Este grupo llevó a las colonias a la **independencia**.

THE NEW UNITED STATES

Benjamin Franklin played a big part in forming the new United States. In 1776, he helped write the **Declaration of Independence**.

In 1779, Franklin was named U.S. **ambassador** to France. He held the job until 1785, when he returned to the United States and helped write the **Constitution**.

In this painting, Franklin (left) works on the Declaration of Independence with John Adams (center) and Thomas Jefferson (right).

En esta pintura, Franklin (izquierda) trabaja en la Declaración de la Independencia con John Adams (centro) y Thomas Jefferson (derecha).

Franklin got France to help the colonies fight Great Britain in the American Revolution. This picture shows him in France.

Franklin convenció a Francia para que ayudara a las colonias en su lucha con la Gran Bretaña. Aquí vemos a Franklin en una visita a Francia.

LOS NUEVOS ESTADOS UNIDOS

Benjamin Franklin jugó un papel importante en la formación de los nuevos Estados Unidos. En 1776, Franklin ayudó a escribir la **Declaración de Independencia**

En 1779, Franklin fue nombrado **embajador** de EE.UU. en Francia. Ocupó el puesto hasta 1785, cuando regresó a los Estados Unidos y ayudó a redactar la **Constitución**.

A Long and Great Life

Benjamin Franklin died on April 17, 1790. He was 84 years old. He was a writer who spoke his mind on the politics of his day.

Franklin was both a world traveler and a man who worked to make his community better. His work can be seen today in the presence of libraries and other public services in every community.

During his life, Franklin was a scientist, an inventor, a politician, and a writer.

Benjamín Franklin murió el 17 de abril de 1790. Tenía 84 años de edad. Franklin fue un escritor que decía lo que pensaba sobre la política de su época.

Franklin fue a la vez un viajero del mundo y un hombre que trabajó para mejorar su comunidad. Su obra se puede ver hoy en bibliotecas y otros servicios públicos de las comunidades.

Franklin fue científico, inventor, político y escritor.

TIMELINE / CRONOLOGÍA

January 17, 1706
17 de enero de 1706

Franklin is born.

Nace Benjamín Franklin.

1718

Franklin begins his printing apprenticeship.

Franklin comienza su aprendizaje como impresor.

1732

Franklin starts *Poor Richard's Almanack*.

Franklin comienza el *Poor Richard's Almanack*.

April 17, 1790
17 de abril de 1790

Franklin dies.

Muere Benjamín Franklin.

1779

Franklin is named U.S. ambassador to France

Franklin es nombrado embajador de los Estados Unidos en Francia.

1757

Franklin is given the job of Colonial agent in London.

Franklin es nombrado representante de las colonias en Londres.

Glossary

ambassador (am-BA-suh-dur) Someone who speaks for his or her country.

American Revolution (uh-MER-uh-ken reh-vuh-LOO-shun) Battles that soldiers from the colonies fought against Britain for freedom, from 1775 to 1783.

apprenticeship (uh-PREN-tis-ship) A period in which a young person works with another person to learn a skill or trade.

citizen (SIH-tih-zen) A person who is born in or has a right to live somewhere.

colonies (KAH-luh-neez) Places where people move that are still ruled by the leaders of the country from which they came.

Constitution (kon-stih-TOO-shun) The basic rules by which the United States is governed.

Continental Congress (kon-tuh-NEN-tul KON-gres) A group, made up of a few people from every colony, that made decisions for the colonies.

Declaration of Independence (deh-kluh-RAY-shun UV in-duh-PEN-dints) An official announcement signed on July 4, 1776, in which American colonists stated they were free of British rule.

French and Indian War (FRENCH AND IN-dee-un WOR) The battles fought between 1754 and 1763 by England, France, and Native Americans for control of North America.

independence (in-dih-PEN-dents) Freedom from the control of other people.

Glosario

aprendizaje (el) Un período en el que una persona joven trabaja con otra persona para aprender un oficio o comercio.

ciudadano, a (el/la) Una persona que nace, o tiene derecho a vivir en algun lugar.

colonias (las) Lugares donde se mueven las personas que aun son gobernados por los líderes del país de donde vinieron.

Congreso Continental (el) Un grupo formado por representantes de las colonias para tomar decisiones.

Constitución (la) Las normas básicas por las que se rigen los Estados Unidos.

Declaración de Independencia (la) El anuncio oficial, firmado el 4 de julio de 1776, en la que colonos americanos declararon que estaban libres de la dominación británica.

embajador, a (el/la) Alguien que representa a su país.

Guerra de Independencia (la) Batallas en las que las Colonias buscaban su libertad de la Gran Bretaña.

Guerra Franco-india (la) Las batallas libradas entre 1754 y 1763 por Inglaterra, Francia, y los nativos americanos para obtener el control de América del Norte.

independencia (la) La libertad del control de otras personas.

Index

A

ambassador, 18, 22
apprenticeship, 6, 10, 22

B

Boston, Massachusetts, 6, 10

C

children, 6, 10
cities, 4

colonies, 8, 14, 16
community, 4, 20
Constitution, 18
Continental Congress, 16

D

Declaration of Independence, 18

F

fire department, 4
French and Indian War, 14

H

hospital, 4

I

inventor, 6

L

library, 4, 20

S

services, 4, 20

W

writer, 6, 20

Índice

A

aprendiz, 7, 11, 22

B

biblioteca, 5, 21
Boston, Massachusetts, 7, 11

C

ciudades, 5
colonias, 9, 15, 17

comunidad, 5, 21
Congreso Continental, 17
Constitución, 19

D

Declaración de Independencia, 19
departamento de bomberos, 5

E

embajador, 19, 22
escritor, 7, 21

G

Guerra Franco-india, 15

H

hijos, 11
hospital, 5

I

inventor, 7

S

servicios, 5, 21

GIRL

Almighty

AN INTERACTIVE JOURNAL

for Being a Mighty Activist of the World

— & OTHER UTTERLY RESPECTABLE PURSUITS —

by

NICOLE LARUE

GIBBS SMITH

TO ENRICH AND INSPIRE HUMANKIND

CHAPTER ONE

AGENT

for Change

AGENT
for Change

....

This chapter favors the brave ones,
the bold ones, the reliably fearless ones,
the ones who choose to daringly speak
out, the mover and the shaker and those
with requisite swagger to rise up.
Learn to show up in your world by knowing
the score, keeping up to date with
goings-on, engaging in your community
at large, staying well informed and being
resolutely wise to that which requires
some shaking up.

Okay, brave one, jump in!

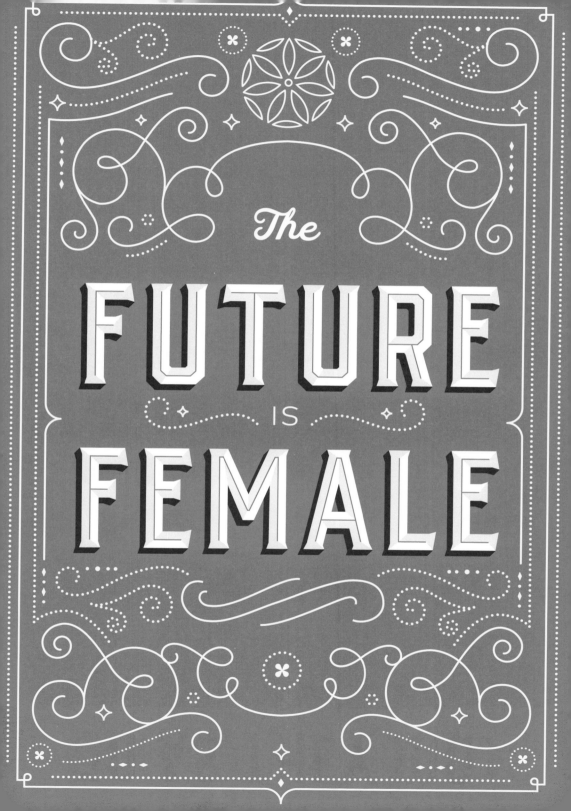

Malala Yousafzai

" WHEN THE WHOLE WORLD IS SILENT,
EVEN ONE VOICE BECOMES POWERFUL. "

....

BORN: July 12, 1997

Job: Activist for Female Education

FACT: From Pakistan

FACT: Was shot by a Taliban gunman

FACT: The youngest person to receive the Nobel Peace Prize

FACT: Named after a famous Afghani poet and warrior

FACT: July 12 was named as "Malala Day" by the United Nations

FACT: She wrote a best-selling book called *I Am Malala*

What's Malala's activist story?

What might your activist story be?

NAME?

Two prominent elected officials
What makes them so ridiculously prominent?

. . . .

. . . .

_____

_____

_____

Two stellar prime ministers
What makes them so ridiculously stellar?

. . . .

. . . .

_____

_____

_____

Two leading political scientists
What makes them such ridiculously good leaders?

. . . .

. . . .

Two powerful activists
What makes them so ridiculously powerful?

. . . .

. . . .

Two masterful public speakers
What makes them so ridiculously masterful?

. . . .

. . . .

DEVISE & CONQUER

Come up with something *DARING* to share with others (an event, a book, an idea, an experience, a film... Get creative, be clever, think unconventionally, use your imagination, develop a vision, take a giant leap, have an innovative mindset, do something mighty!) and then use a crowdfunding method to bring your small and mighty project to life!

PROJECT:

_____

_____

_____

_____

GOAL:

_____

_____

HOW YOU WILL GO ABOUT IT (PLAN, SCHEDULE, BUDGET):

_____   _____

_____   _____

_____   _____

WHY THIS PROJECT? (WHY IS IT IMPORTANT TO YOU AND WHY IS IT IMPORTANT TO SHARE?):

_____

_____

_____

_____

_____

_____

_____

Would you
RATHER?

(circle your answers)

BE RICH **or** FAMOUS?

SPEAK OUT **or** CRAWL INTO YOUR SHELL?

BE A COUNTRY MOUSE **or** A CITY MOUSE?

BE THE BOSS **or** THE EMPLOYEE?

SPEAK IN PUBLIC **or** SING IN PUBLIC?

PLAY A VILLAIN **or** A HEROINE?

BE FAMOUS FOR BEING EXTREMELY INTELLIGENT **or** FOR BEING GOOD LOOKING?

SPEND THE DAY WITH A FAMOUS HISTORICAL FIGURE **or** AN ANCESTOR?

CRY AFTER ANYONE SPEAKS TO YOU **or** LAUGH UNCONTROLLABLY?

MEET YOUR FAVORITE MOVIE STAR **or** THE PRESIDENT OF THE UNITED STATES?

BE ABLE TO SPEAK A FOREIGN LANGUAGE FLUENTLY **or** UNDERSTAND IT?

MARCH IN THE STREETS **or** SIGN MIGHTY DOCUMENTS BEHIND A DESK?

SPEAK YOUR MIND **or** PLAY NICE WITH OTHERS?

WIN THE LOTTERY **or** GET SUPERPOWERS?

BE A TEAM PLAYER **or** A COMMITTEE OF ONE?

RESEARCH FOR DAYS **or** HAVE A GO GET 'EM ATTITUDE?

WIN THE NOBEL PEACE PRIZE **or** AN ACADEMY AWARD?

HEAR LOCAL NEWS **or** INTERNATIONAL OPINIONS?

What questions might you ask a community leader, a powerful speaker or a fellow activist?

Write down six mighty questions and choose a hotshot to interview!

1 _____

_____

_____

_____

2 _____

_____

_____

_____

3 _____

_____

_____

_____

4 _____

_____

_____

_____

5 _____

_____

_____

_____

6 _____

_____

_____

_____

_____

_____

(Look, I get it. We don't all know the rich and the famous, but you can surely reach out to some heavy hitters, some superheroes! Some of these grand humans might be a family member or a teacher or a business owner that you already know. Just remember, confidence is rad, so put some of daring in your back pocket and go for it!)

Brave
SCAVENGER

· · · · · · · · · · · · · · · · · · · ·

Set out on a scavenger hunt!
Take pictures, collect things
& size up your findings!

☐ YOUR TOWN'S OFFICIAL SEAL

Date: Location:

Description: _____

_____

_____

☐ PHOTO OF FRAMED COLLEGE DEGREES
OR PROFESSIONAL CERTIFICATES

Date: Location:

Description: _____

_____

_____

☐ YOUR COUNTRY'S FLAG

Date: Location:

Description: _____

_____

_____

☐ A FLYER FOR A POLITICAL EVENT

Date: Location:

Description: _____

_____

_____

☐ A VOTER REGISTRATION FORM

Date: Location:

Description: _____

_____

_____

☐ A POLITICAL LAWN SIGN

Date: Location:

Description: _____

_____

_____

☐ A PHOTO OF YOU IN FRONT
OF YOUR TOWN HALL

Date: Location:

Description: _____

_____

_____

☐ THE WORD "VOTE"

Date: Location:

Description: _____

_____

_____

☐ THE SYMBOL FOR A POLITICAL PARTY

Date: Location:

Description: _____

_____

_____

☐ THE COVER OF AN ACTIVIST BOOK

Date: Location:

Description: _____

_____

_____

Notes:

_____

_____

_____

_____

Just LISTEN

If you were to write, create, design or start a podcast around the idea of *Political Activism*, what specific issues would excite you the most? Who would be your audience? How do you think your audience would benefit from listening? Write a short podcast pitch that could convince someone of this brilliant idea!

POWERS THAT BE

IDENTIFY AND READ UP ON THE DECISION MAKERS IN YOUR OWN COUNTRY.

Whether it be in your city, community, whistle-stop, state, monarchy, territory, hamlet, principality, kingdom, commonwealth, township, bailiwick, province, county, region, sovereignty, borough, civic, town or neighborhood, they impact you.

Work to understand their role and involvement in your government, system of rule, regime, leadership, higher-up, bureaucracy, empire, powers that be, ruling party, legislature, union, tribe, parliament, upper management, assembly, cabinet, administration, pecking order, high command, league, hierarchy or dictatorship.

Who are they? What do they do? When are they elected, decided upon, voted in? Where do they do their decision making? Why is this role necessary? How might their role impact you?

Decision Maker:

. . . .

_____

_____

_____

_____

Decision Maker:

. . . .

_____

_____

_____

_____

Decision Maker:

. . . .

_____

_____

_____

_____

DICTIONARY IN THE

No. 7

What does *fearlessness* mean to you? How would you define it?
List 10 words you would use to describe fearlessness:

Sing IT! Learn and note another country's anthem or national song. What is the country celebrating? What values is it trying to convey? Is it inspiring to you?

Country: ....

Anthem: ....

_____

_____

_____

_____

_____

_____

_____

_____

_____

_____

_____

_____

_____

_____

_____

_____

_____

_____

_____

_____

_____

_____

Volunteer, VOLUNTEER
VOLUNTEER

Find a **political cause** to commit your time to! Volunteering your time can make all the difference for so many rad purposes in your community and world. Start by listing as many opportunities as you can think of or look up. Decide on one that interests you the very most and write down reasons why you'd be a good fit and how you feel you would make a difference. Then, go get 'em!

- ○ Political party campaign
- ○ League of Women Voters
- ○ Generation Progress
- ○
- ○
- ○
- ○
- ○
- ○
- ○
- ○
- ○
- ○
- ○
- ○
- ○
- ○
- ○
- ○
- ○

REASONS WHY:

_____

_____

_____

_____

_____

_____

_____

_____

_____

_____

_____

_____

_____

_____

_____

_____

_____

_____

_____

Use this page to sketch alternatives for your country's flag. What things would you include that would make you feel proud to be the symbol of your country?

Letter Writer's
REVIVAL

Change things up today and write a letter, a postcard or a quick note to a government official, an out of touch friend or someone you've always found inspiring. Yep, a handwritten (the pen or pencil type) archaic activity. But, just wait and see, the connections are oftentimes the most phenomenal!

Dear _____ ,

_____
_____
_____
_____
_____
_____
_____
_____
_____
_____
_____
_____
_____
_____
_____
_____
_____
_____
_____
_____
_____

ACTIVISM IS...

Everything that made me feel rebellious this week:

BRAVE

Why NOT?

Pick something:

- ○ Make a public speech
- ○ Stand on your soap box
- ○ Write to your senator
- ○ Pass out voter registration information
- ○ Register to vote
- ○ Become a good listener
- ○ Visit your state capitol
- ○ Research voting rights in your state or community
- ○ Do one rebellious thing
- ○ Find ways to promote political education
- ○ Join an activist group
- ○ Read a banned book
- ○ Run for office
- ○ Engage with elected officials (via email, letters, social media...)
- ○ Help out with a campaign
- ○ Find ways to help fight voter suppression in your state
- ○ March in the streets
- ○ Find volunteer opportunities in your own town
- ○ Write a press release
- ○ Read your local news
- ○ Learn about how your government works
- ○ Attend a town hall meeting
- ○ Contribute to someone's political campaign
- ○ Write a protest song
- ○ Educate people on issues that are important to the community
- ○ Participate in social media activist groups

25 THINGS I'VE DISCOVERED WHILE BEING *Brave:*

1. _____
2. _____
3. _____
4. _____
5. _____
6. _____
7. _____
8. _____
9. _____
10. _____
11. _____
12. _____
13. _____
14. _____

15. _____

16. _____

17. _____

18. _____

19. _____

20. _____

21. _____

22. _____

23. _____

24. _____

25. _____

Aha!

As you travel through the world, you're bound to have brilliant realizations, crazy insights and sudden inspiration—if you're open to them. Here's where you can write these things down.

RECORD YOUR AHA MOMENTS & DETERMINE HOW THEY WILL HELP YOU CONTINUE MOVING, ONLY FORWARD!

WELL EARNED *Rebel* BADGES

TROOP#001

Super Rad!

REVOLUTIONARY

FIERCE

— GENTLE —
Rebel

Reformer

— Born —
LEADER

CHAPTER TWO

....

GREEN

Activist

GREEN

Activist

....

This chapter sustains the mighty trailblazers, the enduring stewards, those who are a force of nature and those willing to champion the seemingly impossible. Learn to show up in your world by finding unparalleled ways to conserve, build things up, focus on the essential, encourage growth and be willing to get your hands a little dirty.

All right then, get cracking!

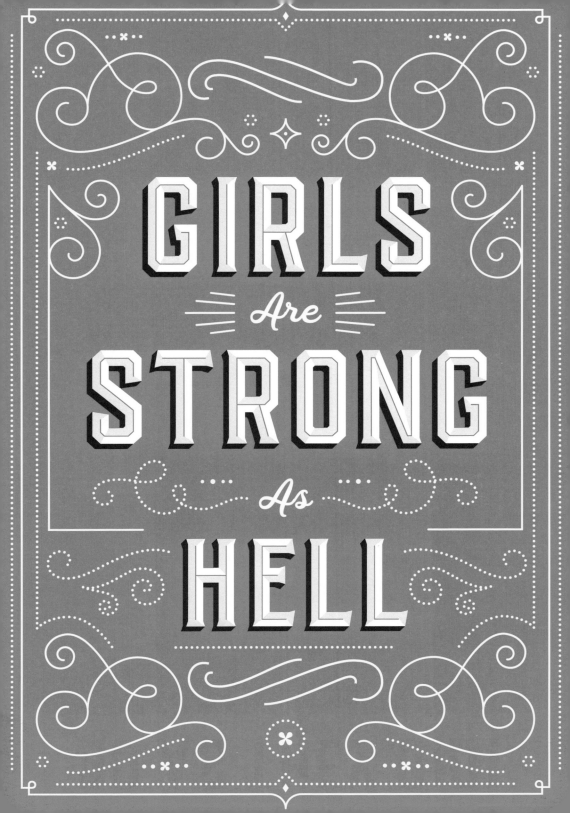

Temple Grandin

"THE MOST IMPORTANT THING PEOPLE DID FOR ME WAS TO EXPOSE ME TO NEW THINGS."

....

BORN: August 29, 1947

Job: Professor of Animal Science

FACT: A spokesperson for autism

FACT: Is the oldest of four children

FACT: Inventor of the Hug Machine

FACT: Didn't start talking until she was 3 ½

FACT: She doesn't think in words, she thinks in pictures

FACT: Wrote a book called *Animals Make Us Human*

What's Temple's stewardship story?

What might your stewardship story be?

_____

_____

_____

_____

_____

_____

_____

_____

_____

_____

_____

_____

_____

_____

_____

CAN YOU NAME?

Two world-changing conservationists
What makes them so ridiculously good stewards?

· ·

· ·

_____

_____

_____

Two superstar environmental activists
What makes them so ridiculously incredible?

· ·

· ·

_____

_____

_____

Two acclaimed green builders
What makes them so ridiculously acclaimed?

. . . .

. . . .

_____

_____

_____

Two celebrated biologists
What makes them so ridiculously celebrated?

. . . .

. . . .

_____

_____

_____

Two brilliant natural scientists
What makes them so ridiculously brilliant?

. . . .

. . . .

_____

_____

_____

DEVISE & CONQUER

(put something out into *your* world)

Come up with something *TRAILBLAZING* to share with others (an event, a book, an idea, an experience, a film... Get creative, be clever, think unconventionally, use your imagination, develop a vision, take a giant leap, have an innovative mindset, do something mighty!) and then use a crowdfunding method to bring your small and mighty project to life!

PROJECT: _____

_____

_____

_____

GOAL: _____

_____

_____

HOW YOU WILL GO ABOUT IT (PLAN, SCHEDULE, BUDGET):

_____   _____

_____   _____

_____   _____

WHY THIS PROJECT? (WHY IS IT IMPORTANT TO YOU AND WHY IS IT IMPORTANT TO SHARE?):

_____

_____

_____

_____

_____

_____

Would you RATHER?

(circle your answers)

SPEND ONE YEAR SAILING AROUND THE WORLD *or* ONE YEAR LIVING IN YOUR FAVOR-ITE FOREIGN COUNTRY?

PLAY INSIDE ALL DAY *or* PLAY OUTSIDE ALL DAY?

LIVE IN A WINDY CITY *or* NEAR A SUNNY BEACH?

BE A BUILDER *or* A GROWER?

DO SOMETHING MEANINGFUL *or* SOMETHING THAT'S HIGHLY CELEBRATED?

HAVE TO ENTER ROOMS BACKWARD *or* ALWAYS HAVE TO SOMERSAULT OUT?

LIVE INSIDE A LIBRARY *or* OUTSIDE IN A NATIONAL PARK?

OWN A ZOO *or* AN ANIMAL SHELTER?

SPEND EVERY MINUTE OF THE REST OF YOUR LIFE OUTSIDE *or* INSIDE?

HAVE THE LIFE OF A DOG *or* THE LIFE OF A CAT?

LIVE IN A HOME WITH NO ELECTRICITY *or* IN A HOME WITH NO RUNNING WATER?

ALWAYS BE TIRED *or* ALWAYS BE HUNGRY?

BE STUNG BY TWELVE BEES *or* A SINGLE WASP?

GO SKYDIVING *or* GO ON A HOT AIR BALLOON RIDE?

BE A DOG TRAINER *or* A WILDCAT TRAINER?

BE A VEGETARIAN FOR THE REST OF YOUR LIFE *or* ONLY BE ABLE TO EAT BACON?

KNOW WHAT ANIMALS ARE THINKING *or* WHAT HUMANS ARE THINKING?

LIVE IN A FIVE-STAR PRISON *or* THE POOREST COUNTRY IN THE WORLD?

What questions might you ask a mighty trailblazer, a celebrated biologist or an environmental activist?

Write down six mighty questions and choose a hotshot to interview!

1

2

3

4 _____

_____

_____

_____

5 _____

_____

_____

_____

6 _____

_____

_____

_____

_____

_____

(Look, I get it. We don't all know the rich and the famous, but you can surely reach out to some heavy hitters, some superheroes! Some of these grand humans might be a family member or a teacher or a business owner that you already know. Just remember, confidence is rad, so put some daring in your back pocket and go for it!)

Natural
SCAVENGER

· · · · · · · · · · · · · · · · · · · ·

Set out on a scavenger hunt!
Take pictures, collect things
& size up your findings!

☐ SOMETHING PLASTIC

Date: Location:

Description: _____
_____
_____

☐ A SOLITARY BIT OF NATURE

Date: Location:

Description: _____
_____
_____

☐ SOME SORT OF WILDLIFE

Date: Location:

Description: _____
_____
_____

☐ SOMETHING THAT FLIES

Date: Location:

Description: _____
_____
_____

☐ SOMETHING YOU CAN ONLY USE OUTDOORS

Date: Location:

Description: _____
_____
_____

☐ A LIVING OBJECT

Date: Location:

Description: _____
_____
_____

☐ BIKE PATH SIGN

Date: Location:

Description: _____
_____
_____

☐ LITTER

Date: Location:

Description: _____
_____
_____

☐ THE WORD "GREEN"

Date: Location:

Description: _____
_____
_____

☐ SEVERAL DIFFERENT RECYCLE SIGNS

Date: Location:

Description: _____
_____
_____

Notes:
_____
_____
_____

Just LISTEN

If you were to write, create, design or start a podcast around the idea of
Environmental Activism, what specific issues would excite you the most?
Who would be your audience? How do you think your audience would benefit
from listening? Write a short podcast pitch that could convince someone of
this brilliant idea!

Guess WHERE?

So you may not yet be a world traveler, but hopefully your curiosity around global cuisine isn't hinging on your overseas excursions. Here's a list of tasty, unusual, noteworthy and curious foods from all over the map! Give a good guess where each of them are from, and if you are having trouble figuring it out, look it up, use your explorer skills and learn more about all of the things you may be missing out on just by not knowing!

1. KIMCHI
2. MEAT PIE
3. PHO
4. STEAK TARTARE
5. APPLE STRUDEL
6. RAMEN
7. MARZIPAN
8. SPAM
9. PUFFER FISH
10. MEZE
11. POUTINE
12. TOM YUM SOUP
13. PIEROGI
14. STEAK & KIDNEY PIE
15. CROISSANT

15. ESCARGOT
17. SQUEAKY CHEESE
18. MAPLE SYRUP
19. BAUMKUCHEN
20. PEKING DUCK
21. AIOLI
22. HUMMUS
23. HAMBURGER
24. SPANAKOPITA
25. MACARON
26. GOULASH
27. KOBE BEEF
28. PAELLA
29. VEGEMITE
30. BULGOGI

Guess Where Answers

1. SOUTH KOREA
2. AUSTRALIA
3. VIETNAM
4. FRANCE
5. AUSTRIA
6. JAPAN
7. GERMANY
8. UNITED STATES
9. JAPAN
10. TURKEY
11. CANADA
12. THAILAND
13. POLAND
14. ENGLAND
15. FRANCE
16. FRANCE
17. FINLAND
18. CANADA
19. GERMANY
20. CHINA
21. FRANCE
22. MIDDLE EAST
23. GERMANY
24. GREECE
25. FRANCE
26. HUNGARY
27. JAPAN
28. SPAIN
29. AUSTRALIA
30. SOUTH KOREA

Always PREPARED

Take steps to be ready to respond and possibly even lend a hand in times of emergency (emergency things could be: flooding, extreme heat, home fires, power outages, drought, earthquakes, hurricanes, landslides, wildfires, severe weather, tornadoes, thunderstorms & lightning...). Make a plan—it's no doubt the simplest way to be at the top of one's game when facing danger!

Key questions to give some thought to:

How do/will I receive emergency alerts?

_____

_____

_____

Where/what are my evacuation routes?

_____

_____

_____

What will my household need?

_____

_____

_____

Checklist:

(write in some of your own!)

- ○ First aid kit
- ○ Water
- ○ Fire extinguisher
- ○ Medical prescriptions
- ○ Names & ages of household members
- ○ Inventory of pets or other animals
- ○ _____
- ○ _____
- ○ _____
- ○ _____
- ○ _____
- ○ _____
- ○ _____
- ○ _____
- ○ _____
- ○ _____
- ○ _____
- ○ _____
- ○ _____
- ○ _____
- ○ _____
- ○ _____
- ○ _____
- ○ _____
- ○ _____
- ○ _____
- ○ _____
- ○ _____
- ○ _____
- ○ _____

STEWARDSHIP IS...

Everything that made me feel like Earth's ambassador this week:

YOUR WORLD

Learn of a building in your community that could benefit from a bit of beautifying. Then gather a team of artists, painters and creatives and plan a mural project for this space! If you don't have the creative skill, be the idea person and make this a trailblazing statement for your community.

WRITE A LIST OR SKETCH YOUR MURAL IDEAS RIGHT HERE, RIGHT NOW:

GREEN READING

Now that you're a part-time community activist, how about taking on a brilliant, local project that will, without a doubt, activate and connect the green-minded people in your community or neighborhood? We're talking Little Free Libraries, people! The raddest of rad, free neighborhood book exchanges. A Little Free Library in your very own neighborhood where everyone can share a book and take a book and encourages reading!

TAKE ACTION:

1. You will need to designate at least one caretaker for your little free library.

2. Find someone locally who might be willing to build your Little Free Library for you OR raise money by getting your neighborhood and community involved.

3. Hold a grand opening and invite your pals, your schoolmates and your comrades-in-arms.

4. Tell everyone about it, scream it from your rooftop (possibly via flyers or social media or local community board). The more support you have in this grand adventure, the better.

PLANNING PAGE:

Every Little Free Library is one of a kind, and yours will be too!
Use this space to start sketching ideas, shapes, and sizes
to help your builder know just what you have in mind.

. . . .

DICTIONARY

IN THE

Not

What does **stewardship** mean to you? How would you define it?
List 10 words you would use to describe stewardship:

Volunteer, VOLUNTEER, VOLUNTEER

Find an **environmental cause** to commit your time to! Volunteering your time can make all the difference for so many rad purposes in your community and world. Start by listing as many as you can think of or look up. Decide on one that interests you the very most and write down reasons why you'd be a good fit and how you feel you would make a difference. Then, go get 'em!!

- ○ Community Gardens
- ○ Animal Shelters
- ○ Park, River or Beach Clean Up
- ○ _____
- ○ _____
- ○ _____
- ○ _____
- ○ _____
- ○ _____
- ○ _____
- ○ _____
- ○ _____
- ○ _____
- ○ _____
- ○ _____
- ○ _____
- ○ _____
- ○ _____
- ○ _____
- ○ _____
- ○ _____
- ○ _____

- ○ _____
- ○ _____
- ○ _____
- ○ _____
- ○ _____
- ○ _____
- ○ _____
- ○ _____
- ○ _____
- ○ _____
- ○ _____
- ○ _____
- ○ _____
- ○ _____
- ○ _____
- ○ _____
- ○ _____
- ○ _____
- ○ _____
- ○ _____
- ○ _____
- ○ _____

DO ONE THING EVERY DAY
THAT IS

MEANINGFUL

- ○ Leave your digital devices at home
- ○ Start your own recycling club
- ○ Avoid buying anything new for a month
- ○ Join an animal rights group
- ○ Volunteer for community clean up days
- ○ Boycott goods that use animal testing
- ○ Plan a demonstration for something you believe in
- ○ Set up recycling stations at your local community center
- ○ Tend a booth during an Earth Day celebration
- ○ Write a letter to your local newspaper
- ○ Volunteer in an environmental campaign
- ○ Find volunteer opportunities in our national parks
- ○ Research the environmental laws in your state or community
- ○ Do one thing for the environment today
- ○ Research the activities of The Sierra Club
- ○ Consider raising a puppy to be a search and rescue dog
- ○ Learn about ways to help conserve energy
- ○ Volunteer at an animal shelter or sanctuary
- ○ Try being a vegetarian for a month
- ○ Engage in community service
- ○ Find ways to help with pollution prevention
- ○ Do some guerrilla gardening (like dropping wildflower seeds in park strips)
- ○ Picket at a particular factory you oppose

THINGS I'VE DISCOVERED DURING MY Travels:

1.

2.

3.

4.

5.

6.

7.

8.

9.

10.

11.

12.

13.

14.

15. _____

16. _____

17. _____

18. _____

19. _____

20. _____

21. _____

22. _____

23. _____

24. _____

25. _____

Aha!

As you travel through the world, you're bound to have brilliant realizations, crazy insights and sudden inspiration—if you're open to them. Here's where you can write these things down.

RECORD YOUR AHA MOMENTS & DETERMINE HOW THEY WILL HELP YOU CONTINUE MOVING, ONLY FORWARD!

WELL EARNED Rebel BADGES

OFFICIAL TREE HUGGER

Magic!

SUPERHERO

MIGHTY **TRAIL** BLAZER

— GREEN —
Goddess

Wild — AND — **FREE**

>> *Effin'* <<
BRILLIANT

CHAPTER THREE

....

GLOBAL

Anthropologist

GLOBAL
Anthropologist

....

This chapter supports team players, the truly daring reporters, the bona fide and unwavering, the staunchly resolute ones and those with adventure enough in their hearts to move things forward.
Learn to show up in your world by keeping the peace, traveling near and far, finding common ground and acting as ambassador for the people.

Now, go get 'em!

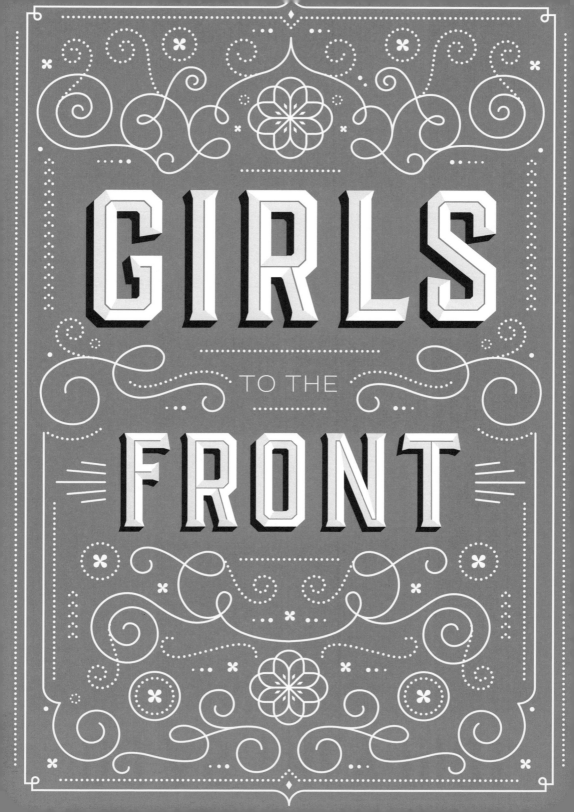

Brené Brown

"SOMETIMES THE BRAVEST AND MOST IMPORTANT THING YOU CAN DO IS JUST SHOW UP."

··

BORN: November 18, 1965

Job: Storyteller, Research Professor, Author, Public Speaker

FACT: Author of five #1 *New York Times* best sellers

FACT: Does not believe cursing and praying are mutually exclusive

FACT: Gave one of the top five most viewed TED Talks in the world

FACT: Did a seven-year study on courage and leadership

FACT: Has two children

FACT: Is the CEO for The Daring Way™ program

What's Brené's adventurer story?

What might your adventurer story be?

_____

_____

_____

_____

_____

_____

_____

_____

_____

_____

_____

_____

_____

_____

_____

NAME?

Two adventurous travel writers
What makes them so ridiculously adventurous?

. . . .

. . . .

_____

_____

_____

Two impressive international aid workers
What makes them so ridiculously impressive?

. . . .

. . . .

_____

_____

_____

Two insightful behavior analysts
What makes them so ridiculously insightful?

. . . .

. . . .

_____

_____

_____

Two daring reporters
What makes them so ridiculously daring?

. . . .

. . . .

_____

_____

_____

Two brilliant ambassadors
What makes them so ridiculously brilliant?

. . . .

. . . .

_____

_____

_____

DEVISE & CONQUER

(put something out into your world)

Come up with something *ADVENTUROUS* to share with others (an event, a book, an idea, an experience, a film... Get creative, be clever, think unconventionally, use your imagination, develop a vision, take a giant leap, have an innovative mindset, do something mighty!) and then use a crowdfunding method to bring your small and mighty project to life!

PROJECT:

GOAL:

HOW YOU WILL GO ABOUT IT (PLAN, SCHEDULE, BUDGET):

WHY THIS PROJECT? (WHY IS IT IMPORTANT TO YOU AND WHY IS IT IMPORTANT TO SHARE?):

Would you

RATHER?

(circle your answers)

BE INVISIBLE *or* BE ABLE TO FLY?

BE COMPLETELY ALONE FOR 5 YEARS *or* NEVER ALONE FOR 5 YEARS?

NEVER TOUCH AN ELECTRONIC DEVICE AGAIN *or* NEVER TOUCH A HUMAN AGAIN?

REPORT THE NEWS *or* BE THE ONE WHO DISCOVERS THE NEWS?

BE SOMETIMES DARING *or* ALWAYS PEACEFUL?

STOP HUMAN TRAFFICKING *or* END WORLD HUNGER?

BE A BRILLIANT WRITER WITH NO PUBLISHED BOOKS *or* A CRAPPY WRITER WITH ONLY ONE PUBLISHED BOOK?

HAVE THE POWER TO END WAR IN THE WORLD *or* THE POWER TO END POVERTY?

BE ABLE TO HEAR ANY CONVERSATION *or* TAKE BACK ANYTHING YOU SAY?

READ A BOOK WITH THE LAST PAGE MISSING *or* LEAVE A MOVIE EARLY?

KEEP A DAILY JOURNAL *or* A DAILY SKETCHBOOK?

VISIT ANOTHER COUNTRY *or* LEARN ANOTHER LANGUAGE?

BE AN AMBASSADOR FOR YOUR COUNTRY *or* REPORT YOUR COUNTRY'S NEWS?

LIVE THE REST OF YOUR LIFE IN ANOTHER COUNTRY *or* NEVER BE ABLE TO TRAVEL?

LIVE WHEREVER YOU WANT FOR FREE *or* TRAVEL WHEREVER YOU WANT FOR FREE?

GO TO JAIL FOR A YEAR *or* BE HOMELESS FOR A YEAR?

What questions might you ask an anthropologist, a daring reporter or an adventurous travel writer?

Write down six mighty questions and choose a hotshot to interview!

1

2

3

4

5

6

(Look, I get it. We don't all know the rich and the famous, but you can surely reach out to some heavy hitters, some superheroes! Some of these grand humans might be a family member or a teacher or a business owner that you already know. Just remember, confidence is rad, so put some of daring in your back pocket and go for it!)

World
SCAVENGER

· · · · · · · · · · · · · · · · · · · ·

Set out on a scavenger hunt!
Take pictures, collect things
& size up your findings!

☐ THE FRONT PAGE OF A NEWSPAPER

Date: Location:

Description: _____

_____

_____

☐ A BILL OR COIN OF A FOREIGN CURRENCY

Date: Location:

Description: _____

_____

_____

☐ A PHOTO WITH AS MANY PEOPLE
BORN IN DIFFERENT DECADES

Date: Location:

Description: _____

_____

_____

☐ A SNACK FROM ANOTHER COUNTRY

Date: Location:

Description: _____

_____

_____

☐ A CHANGE OF ADDRESS FORM
FROM THE POST OFFICE

Date: Location:

Description: _____

_____

_____

☐ A PASSPORT PHOTO SHOP

Date: Location:

Description: _____

_____

_____

☐ A NEWS CHANNEL VAN

Date: Location:

Description: _____

_____

_____

☐ A FLYER FOR A FOREIGN EXCHANGE PROGRAM

Date: Location:

Description: _____

_____

_____

☐ A FOREIGN FOODS MARKET OR GROCERY STORE

Date: Location:

Description: _____

_____

_____

☐ THE WORD "GLOBAL"

Date: Location:

Description: _____

_____

_____

Notes:

_____

_____

_____

Just LISTEN

If you were to write, create, design or start a podcast around the idea of *Global Activism*, what specific issues would excite you the most? Who would be your audience? How do you think your audience would benefit from listening? Write a short podcast pitch that could convince someone of this brilliant idea!

_____

_____

_____

_____

_____

_____

_____

_____

_____

_____

_____

_____

_____

_____

_____

_____

_____

_____

_____

_____

_____

_____

_____

_____

_____

Oh, HALLO!

Connecting with people can make all the difference in how you interact with your world and can be as easy as saying *hello*. Trust me, even in trying to speak someone else's language, you'll find brilliant and wondrous ways to connect. So try it out, learn a handful of these, a couple of these, or all of these and put yourself in situations where you can try them out!

FINNISH: HEI

JAPANESE: KONNICHIWA

TURKISH: MERHABA

KOREAN: ANYOUNG HASEYO

SPANISH: HOLA

FRENCH: BONJOUR

ITALIAN: CIAO

HEBREW: SHALOM

GERMAN: HALLO

HUNGARIAN: SZIA

CHINESE: NI HAO

BULGARIAN: ZDRAVEÎTE

THAI: SAWASDEE

CZECH: AHOJ

ARABIC: ASALAAM ALAIKUM

CROATIAN: DOBAR DAN

HINDI: NAMASTE

YIDDISH: A GUTN TOG

RUSSIAN: PRIVET

SWAHILI: HUJAMBO

COMMONWEALTH

Research as many community resources in your town that your mighty brain can come up with. Draw a map of your area and where these resources can be found. It might just come in handy some day!

Think about including:

HEALTH FACILITIES   FIRE & SAFETY   FOOD PANTIRES
PARKS   TOWN HALL   CO-OP GROCERS
LIBRARY   CIVIC CENTERS   JUSTICE DEPTS
PUBLIC POOLS   SHELTERS

A GIRL'S Life

Imagine how other girls live around the world. Choose one country and do a bit of probing! Research, find things out, scout about, delve into things and leave no stone unturned. What is it like to be a girl from this country? Try thinking about things in these broader ways:

Disparities/Inequities: _____

_____

_____

Education: _____

_____

_____

Employment: _____

_____

_____

Economics: _____

_____

_____

Health: _____

_____

_____

Human Rights: _____

_____

_____

Are women's roles in your own country different than theirs?

_____

_____

_____

_____

Why do you think women are often still not afforded
equal respect in many cultures?

_____

_____

_____

_____

Are there changes you would like to see in girls' roles
and rights as you enter adulthood?

_____

_____

_____

_____

What does *daring* mean to you? How would you define it?
List 10 words you would use to describe daring:

PEACE IS...

Everything that made me feel steady this week:

Peace TREATY

Write an imaginary peace treaty between two countries you think might benefit from such a plan. Or construct a treaty between you and a pal or even an agreement between members of your family. Peace treaties can be a remarkable means for ending conflict and repairing regrettable circumstances. Give it a try, see what happens!

This treaty and pact was signed on:

_____ at _____ by two independent parties _____ and _____ .

In order to promote mutual cooperation and enact great peace and security:

by the acceptance and obligation not to resort to _____ or petty _____ (s), by the rule of _____ , _____ and _____ relations with one another, by the inexorable understanding of good social etiquette and emotionally intelligent relationships with one another, agree to this Treaty of Independent Parties.

Article 1. The members of Independent Parties shall cooperate without reservation to this treaty. Any member, after one years' notice of its intention to withdraw from the Party, all its obligations under this treaty shall remain fulfilled at the time of withdrawal.

Article 2. The members shall meet from time to time as occasion may require.

Article 3. Any _____ or threat of _____ , whether immediately affecting any of the members of Independent Parties or not, is hereby declared a matter of concern. In case any such emergency should arise, one or more members may summon a meeting of all members. It is declared to be a friendly right of each member to bring to attention any circumstance whatever affecting good understanding between members upon which _____ depends.

Done in _____ , on the _____ day of _____ , _____ at ____ o'clock.

Member Signature / Seal: _____

Member Signature / Seal: _____

Find a *global cause* to commit your time to! Volunteering your time can make all the difference for so many rad purposes in your community and world. Start by listing as many opportunities as you can think of or look up. Decide on one that interests you the very most and write down reasons why you'd be a good fit and how you feel you would make a difference. Then, go get 'em!!

○ WWOOF
○ Help Exchange
○ Peace Corps

REASONS WHY:

DARING

DO ONE THING EVERY DAY
THAT MAKES YOU

Why NOT?

Pick something:

- ○ Find a foreign pen pal
- ○ Help out with a food drive
- ○ Volunteer at your local community center
- ○ Donate your time at a homeless shelter or soup kitchen
- ○ Write a speech you might give to the United Nations
- ○ Donate books to your local library
- ○ Research programs through Amnesty International
- ○ Send aid packages to places in crisis
- ○ Research human rights in your state or community
- ○ Find volunteer opportunities abroad
- ○ Join a global activities group
- ○ Become a student ambassador
- ○ Read about international news
- ○ Learn more about the Peace Corps
- ○ Do one thing that supports peacekeeping today
- ○ Head a community reading program
- ○ Volunteer your time to help children with disabilities feel better
- ○ Find ways to help out a low-income family
- ○ Research the idea of collective behavior
- ○ Boycott goods produced with slave labor
- ○ Read a book about an international political figure
- ○ Take a course in emergency preparation
- ○ Do something using non-violent resistance
- ○ Become a human rights activist

25 THINGS I'VE DISCOVERED WHILE BEING A *Peacekeeper*:

1. _____

2. _____

3. _____

4. _____

5. _____

6. _____

7. _____

8. _____

9. _____

10. _____

11. _____

12. _____

13. _____

14. _____

15. _____

16. _____

17. _____

18. _____

19. _____

20. _____

21. _____

22. _____

23. _____

24. _____

25. _____

Aha!

As you travel through the world, you're bound to have brilliant realizations, crazy insights and sudden inspiration—if you're open to them. Here's where you can write these things down.

RECORD YOUR AHA MOMENTS & DETERMINE HOW THEY WILL HELP YOU CONTINUE MOVING, ONLY FORWARD!

WELL EARNED Rebel BADGES

GIRL ★ ALMIGHTY

Dang Good

WOMAN KIND

-UNITED-

-MIGHTY- Scout

Braveheart

Going PLACES

CHAPTER FOUR

YOUNG

Feminist

YOUNG
Feminist

....

This chapter champions the fiercely independent, the wild feminist, the female superheroes, the women of action and the dynamo interested in standing up and speaking out.

Learn to show up in your world by speaking with surety, commanding confidence in a crowd, standing for something, championing others and being willing to make people feel just a little bit uncomfortable.

Ready then? March on!

Lindy West

"WOMEN ARE AN ARMY."

....

BORN: March 9, 1982

Job: Writer, Comedian, Activist

FACT: Is a contributing opinion writer for the *New York Times*

FACT: Won the Stranger Genius Award in Literature

FACT: Dislikes "big" as a euphemism

FACT: Is the author of *Shrill: Notes from a Loud Woman*

FACT: She writes a weekly column on feminism and popular culture

FACT: Has helped shift mainstream attitudes about body image

What's Lindy's superhero story?

What might your superhero story be?

Two famed feminists
What makes them so ridiculously famous?

. . . .

. . . .

_____

_____

_____

Two sassy educators
What makes them so ridiculously sassy?

. . . .

. . . .

_____

_____

_____

Two remarkable midwives
What makes them so ridiculously remarkable?

....

....

_____

_____

_____

Two take-charge nonprofit directors
What makes them so ridiculously take-charge?

....

....

_____

_____

_____

Two dedicated foundation organizers
What makes them so ridiculously dedicated?

....

....

_____

_____

_____

DEVISE & CONQUER

Come up with something *AUDACIOUS* to share with others (an event, a book, an idea, an experience, a film... Get creative, be clever, think unconventionally, use your imagination, develop a vision, take a giant leap, have an innovative mindset, do something mighty!) and then use a crowdfunding method to bring your small and mighty project to life!

PROJECT:

GOAL:

HOW YOU WILL GO ABOUT IT (PLAN, SCHEDULE, BUDGET):

WHY THIS PROJECT? (WHY IS IT IMPORTANT TO YOU AND WHY IS IT IMPORTANT TO SHARE?):

Would you

RATHER?

(circle your answers)

NEVER PLAY *or* ALWAYS LOSE?

HAVE TO SHOUT EVERYTHING YOU SAY *or* WHISPER EVERYTHING YOU SAY?

STAY FOREVER AT YOUR CURRENT AGE *or* BE 10 YEARS YOUNGER?

LIVE A LONG LIFE IN POVERTY *or* A SHORT LIFE WITH WEALTH?

LIVE TO BE 1,000 *or* LIVE 10 DIFFERENT LIVES THAT LAST 100 YEARS EACH?

SUFFER FROM SPONTANEOUS SHOUTING *or* UNPREDICTABLE FAINTING SPELLS?

LOSE 5 FRIENDS *or* GAIN 1 ENEMY?

BE ABLE TO SING LIKE A DIVA *or* BE ABLE TO PLAY THE GUITAR LIKE A ROCK STAR?

BE STRANDED ON AN ISLAND WITH SOMEONE YOU HATE *or* STRANDED ON AN ISLAND ALONE?

NEVER BE ABLE TO SAY WHAT'S ON YOUR MIND *or* ALWAYS HAVE TO SPEAK THE TRUTH?

CONTINUE WITH YOUR LIFE *or* RESTART YOUR LIFE?

AGE ONLY FROM THE NECK UP *or* ONLY FROM THE NECK DOWN?

HAVE AN ARRANGED MARRIAGE *or* SPEND THE REST OF YOUR LIFE SINGLE?

WEAR CLOWN MAKEUP EVERY DAY FOR A YEAR *or* WEAR A TUTU EVERY DAY FOR A YEAR?

BE THE MOST INTELLIGENT PERSON AND DO SOMETHING GREAT *or* THE MOST POPULAR PERSON AND DO NOTHING IMPORTANT?

HAVE ONLY TWO CLOSE FRIENDS *or* MANY ACQUAINTANCES?

What questions might you ask a nonprofit director, a brilliant midwife or a famed feminist?

Write down six mighty questions and choose a hotshot to interview!

1

2

3

4 _____

_____

_____

_____

5 _____

_____

_____

_____

6 _____

_____

_____

_____

_____

(Look, I get it. We don't all know the rich and the famous, but you can surely reach out to some heavy hitters, some superheroes! Some of these grand humans might be a family member or a teacher or a business owner that you already know. Just remember, confidence is rad, so put some of daring in your back pocket and go for it!)

Young SCAVENGER

· · · · · · · · · · · · · · · · · · · ·

Set out on a scavenger hunt!
Take pictures, collect things
& size up your findings!

☐ A COLLEGE OR UNIVERSITY

Date: Location:

Description: _____

_____

_____

☐ YOUR REFLECTION

Date: Location:

Description: _____

_____

_____

☐ A CROWD OF PEOPLE

Date: Location:

Description: _____

_____

_____

☐ A PHOTO WITH A WOMAN WHO COULD
HAVE BEEN A SUFFRAGETTE

Date: Location:

Description: _____

_____

_____

☐ A BANNED BOOK

Date: Location:

Description: _____

_____

_____

☐ THE WORD "GIRL"

Date: Location:

Description: _____

_____

_____

☐ A WOMAN EMPOWERMENT BUMPER STICKER

Date: Location:

Description: _____

_____

_____

☐ THE WORD "NO"

Date: Location:

Description: _____

_____

_____

☐ A FEMALE PROFESSOR

Date: Location:

Description: _____

_____

_____

☐ THE COVER OF A FEMINIST BOOK

Date: Location:

Description: _____

_____

_____

Notes:

_____

_____

_____

Just LISTEN

If you were to write, create, design or start a podcast around the idea of *Feminist Activism*, what specific issues would excite you the most? Who would be your audience? How do you think your audience would benefit from listening? Write a short podcast pitch that could convince someone of this brilliant idea!

TODAY!

Today I'm excited about _____

Today I'm excited about _____

Today I'm excited about _____

Today I'm excited about _____

Today I'm excited about _____

Today I'm excited about _____

Today I'm excited about _____

Today I'm excited about _____

Today I'm excited about _____

Today I'm excited about _____

Today I'm excited about _____

Today I'm excited about _____

Today I'm excited about _____

Today I'm excited about _____

Today I'm excited about _____

Today I'm excited about _____

Today I'm excited about _____

Today I'm excited about _____

Today I'm excited about _____

Today I'm excited about _____

MARCH

On

Get clever! Design your own march, rally or activist event T-shirts for your friends or community. Have them say something, be witty and make people feel just a little bit uncomfortable.

Start your sketches here:

INDEPENDENCE IS...

Everything that made me feel empowered this week:

FANGIRLING

Be your own fangirl! Leave notes in random places reminding yourself how awesome you are!

(cut on dotted lines)

Reading
IS
RAD

Write down a list of ten books a girl your age would benefit from reading. Include reasons why you think they're a worthwhile read! Maybe you want to make copies of your list and leave them around (at your school, your place of worship, your local library) for others to find!

Title: ....

Author: ....

_____

Title: ....

Author: ....

_____

Title: ....

Author: ....

_____

Title: ....

Author: ....

_____

Title: ....

Author: ....

_____

Title: ....

Author: ....

_____

Title: ....

Author: ....

_____

Title: ....

Author: ....

_____

Title: ....

Author: ....

_____

Title: ....

Author: ....

_____

DO ONE THING EVERY DAY
THAT MAKES YOU

CONFIDENT

DAILY PEP TALKS

Write down a personal mantra or affirmative statement (you can use your own words, a great quote or piece from a favorite poem) that reminds you of how strong and brilliant and capable you are in this world.

Spirit RAISING

Devise a list of rally cheers, march chants or crowd shouts that you would be proud to stand behind! Here are some already-existing examples:

"Blacks, Latinos, Asians, Whites. We all stand up for human rights!"

"No more pain, no more violence, no more hate, Women Liberate!"

"Hey, hey! Ho, ho! Sexism has got to go!"

"When women's rights are under attack, what do we do? Stand up, fight back!"

"I'm smart! I'm down! I represent my town!"

RESISTANCE!

Talk to women from different generations (women in your family, a school,
a religious community, a senior care facility, at your local watering hole...)
about what rights women were fighting for when they were your age.
These fights don't have to be monumental to count. Remember, things
that are small are often the most mighty!

Create a bullet list of all the brave feats:

-
-
-
-
-
-
-
-
-
-
-
-
-
-
-
-
-
-
-
-
-
-
-
-

- ○ Start an all-girls club
- ○ Write letters to female politicians
- ○ Donate school supplies for girls in less educated countries
- ○ Take to the streets, participate in a protest march
- ○ Find ways to educate others about modern feminists
- ○ Teach young women karate or self defense
- ○ Help start a women's music festival
- ○ Create protest march posters
- ○ Become involved in a Gay-Straight Alliance group
- ○ Boycott businesses that aren't in line with your beliefs
- ○ Volunteer at a women's festival
- ○ Read a book by a feminist author
- ○ Join the League of Women Voters
- ○ Do one thing that supports other women today
- ○ Start a banned book reading group
- ○ Find volunteer opportunities for a local women's organization
- ○ Attend a self defense class
- ○ Join a feminist group
- ○ Advocate for inclusive policies and laws
- ○ Do an interview with a woman in leadership
- ○ Find ways to raise feminist consciousness

25 THINGS I'VE DISCOVERED AS A *Feminist:*

1.
2.
3.
4.
5.
6.
7.
8.
9.
10.
11.
12.
13.
14.

15. _____
_____

16. _____
_____

17. _____
_____

18. _____
_____

19. _____
_____

20. _____
_____

21. _____
_____

22. _____
_____

23. _____
_____

24. _____
_____

25. _____
_____
_____
_____
_____
_____
_____
_____

Aha!

As you travel through the world, you're bound to have brilliant realizations, crazy insights and sudden inspiration—if you're open to them. Here's where you can write these things down.

RECORD YOUR AHA MOMENTS & DETERMINE HOW THEY WILL HELP YOU CONTINUE MOVING, ONLY FORWARD!

WELL EARNED *Rebel* BADGES

REBEL ★ GIRL

SELF
LOVE
CLUB

Brilliant!

LEGENDARY

CHIEF
Feminist
OFFICER

FULL-TIME
Feminist

GIRLFRIEND
Collective

CHAPTER FIVE

·············

CHAMPION

EQUALITY

CHAMPION
for Gender Equality

....

This chapter backs the first-rate players, the inexhaustible workhorses, the ones doing all the cheering and the fireballs prepared to ride shotgun for equality. Learn to show up in your world by recognizing difference, remaining conscientious in things unmatched, fierceley championing the unequal and being a representative for those being driven outside the pack.

This time, play for keeps!

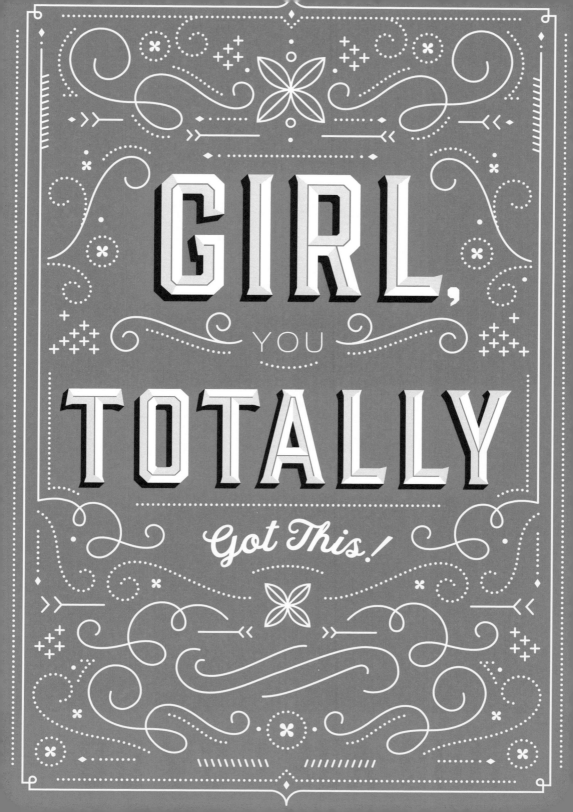

Iris Apfel

" NEVER BE AFRAID TO STOP TRAFFIC."

....

BORN: August 29, 1921

Job: American businesswoman, interior designer, fashion icon

FACT: Is an only child

FACT: Attended art school at the University of Wisconsin

FACT: Worked on design restoration projects for nine U.S. presidents

FACT: Listed as one of the fifty "Best-Dressed over 50"

FACT: Published the book *Iris Apfel: Accidental Icon*

FACT: Is the star of a documentary film called *Iris*

What's Iris's fireball story?

What might your fireball story be?

Two first-rate executive directors
What makes them so ridiculously first-rate?

· ·

· ·

_____

_____

_____

Two notable authors
What makes them so ridiculously notable?

· ·

· ·

_____

_____

_____

Two prominent female empowerment speakers
What makes them so ridiculously prominent?

. . . .

. . . .

_____

_____

_____

Two fierce LGBTQ activists
What makes them so ridiculously fierce?

. . . .

. . . .

_____

_____

_____

Two awe-inspiring mentors
What makes them so ridiculously awe-inspiring?

. . . .

. . . .

_____

_____

_____

DEVISE & CONQUER

(put something out into your world)

Come up with something *FIERCE* to share with others (an event, a book, an idea, an experience, a film... Get creative, be clever, think unconventionally, use your imagination, develop a vision, take a giant leap, have an innovative mindset, do something mighty!) and then use a crowdfunding method to bring your small and mighty project to life!

PROJECT: _____

_____

_____

_____

_____

GOAL: _____

_____

_____

HOW YOU WILL GO ABOUT IT (PLAN, SCHEDULE, BUDGET):

_____   _____

_____   _____

_____   _____

WHY THIS PROJECT? (WHY IS IT IMPORTANT TO YOU AND WHY
IS IT IMPORTANT TO SHARE?):

_____

_____

_____

_____

_____

_____

_____

_____

Would you
RATHER?

(circle your answers)

ALWAYS BE TWENTY MINUTES EARLY *or* TWENTY MINUTES LATE?

FREEZE TIME *or* SHAPE-SHIFT?

LOSE HALF YOUR HEARING *or* HALF YOUR SEEING?

HAVE YOUR GRANDMOTHER'S HAIRSTYLE *or* HER FIRST NAME?

NOT BE ABLE TO READ *or* NOT BE ABLE TO WRITE?

BE RICH *or* FAMOUS?

LIVE ONE HUNDRED YEARS IN THE FUTURE *or* ONE HUNDRED YEARS IN THE PAST?

LIVE A LONG LIFE IN POVERTY *or* A SHORT LIFE WITH WEALTH?

STAY AT YOUR CURRENT AGE FOREVER *or* BE TEN YEARS YOUNGER?

NEVER PLAY *or* ALWAYS LOSE?

HAVE HANDS INSTEAD OF FEET *or* FEET INSTEAD OF HANDS?

HAVE MORE TIME *or* MORE MONEY?

BE THE BEST PLAYER ON A LOSING TEAM *or* THE WORST PLAYER ON A WINNING TEAM?

GET UP VERY EARLY *or* STAY UP VERY LATE?

NOT USE YOUR COMPUTER FOR A MONTH *or* NOT EAT JUNK FOOD FOR A MONTH?

BE VERY SHORT *or* EXTREMELY TALL?

What questions might you ask an executive director, a prominent female speaker or a notable author?

Write down six mighty questions and choose a hotshot to interview!

1 _____

_____

_____

_____

_____

2 _____

_____

_____

_____

_____

3 _____

_____

_____

_____

_____

4

_____

_____

_____

_____

5

_____

_____

_____

_____

6

_____

_____

_____

_____

_____

_____

_____

(Look, I get it. We don't all know the rich and the famous, but you can surely reach out to some heavy hitters, some superheroes! Some of these grand humans might be a family member or a teacher or a business owner that you already know. Just remember, confidence is rad, so put some of daring in your back pocket and go for it!)

☐ A POSTER FOR A PROMINENT
WOMEN'S SPEAKING EVENT
Date: Location:
Description:
_____
_____

☐ AN EQUALITY STICKER
Date: Location:
Description:
_____
_____

☐ A POLITICAL SIGN FOR A FEMALE CANDIDATE
Date: Location:
Description:
_____
_____

☐ A PROFESSIONAL MAGAZINE COVER
FEATURING A WOMAN
Date: Location:
Description:
_____
_____

☐ A RAINBOW FLAG AT A PLACE OF WORSHIP
Date: Location:
Description:
_____
_____

☐ A GENDER-NEUTRAL PUBLIC BATHROOM SIGN
Date: Location:
Description:
_____

☐ A FEMALE-RUN LAW FIRM
Date: Location:
Description:
_____
_____

☐ A FLYER FROM A LOCAL PRIDE CENTER
Date: Location:
Description:
_____
_____

☐ THE WORD "EQUALITY"
Date: Location:
Description:
_____
_____

☐ THE WORD "MATRIARCHY"
Date: Location:
Description:
_____
_____

Notes:
_____
_____
_____

Just LISTEN

If you were to write, create, design or start a podcast around the idea of *Gender-based Activism*, what specific issues would excite you the most? Who would be your audience? How do you think your audience would benefit from listening? Write a short podcast pitch that could convince someone of this brilliant idea!

A GIRL Thing

Take a look at this list of career possibilities and decide whether you think each is a girl thing or a boy thing:

_____	Computer programmer	_____	Principal
_____	Engineer	_____	Facilities manager
_____	Lawyer	_____	Nonprofit director
_____	Reporter	_____	Musician
_____	Scientist	_____	Writer
_____	Dancer	_____	Event planner
_____	Teacher	_____	Artist
_____	Mathematician	_____	Botanist
_____	Biologist	_____	Nanny
_____	Politician	_____	Midwife
_____	Veterinarian	_____	Neurosurgeon
_____	Judge	_____	Travel writer
_____	Pediatrician	_____	Park ranger
_____	Barber	_____	Urban planner
_____	CEO	_____	Architect
_____	Ski instructor	_____	President
_____	Senator	_____	News anchor
_____	Professor		

MAYBE WE CAN SPEND SOME TIME UNPACKING THIS TOGETHER?

Do you believe that any of them are just girl or just boy things?

_____
_____
_____
_____
_____
_____
_____

Do you think any of your responses are based on a gender stereotype?

_____
_____
_____
_____
_____
_____
_____

Where do these ideas come from?

_____
_____
_____
_____
_____
_____
_____

If you had been born into another culture, in another place, were another race or were in a different economic class, what do you suppose your life would look like? *Write that story:*

CAREER *Happiness*

Rate these things 1-14:

_____ Salary

_____ Work content

_____ Meaningfulness

_____ Work flexibility

_____ Job security

_____ Work conditions

_____ Coworker relationships

_____ Advancement

_____ Prestige

_____ Work-life balance

_____ Challenge

_____ Skills

_____ Autonomy

_____ Learning

EQUALITY IS...

Everything that made me feel like I belong this week:

What does *equality* mean to you? How would you define it?
List 10 words you would use to describe equality:

Volunteer, VOLUNTEER

Find a **women-based cause** to commit your time to! Volunteering your time can make all the difference for so many rad purposes in your community and world. Start by listing as many opportunities as you can think of or look up. Decide on one that interests you the very most and write down reasons why you'd be a good fit and how you feel you would make a difference. Then, go get 'em!!

○ YWCA

○ Girls Inc.

○ Futures Without Violence

○ _____

○ _____

○ _____

○ _____

○ _____

○ _____

○ _____

○ _____

○ _____

○ _____

○ _____

○ _____

○ _____

○ _____

○ _____

○ _____

○ _____

○ _____

○ _____

REASONS WHY:

WRITE *it* DOWN

Write a letter to the editor of your local newspaper, favorite news magazine or podcast about an issue you're concerned about that affects you or your community. When you write, be bold but polite, be open and full of conviction and be truly and curiously passionate!

To: _____

Issue: _____

Action: _____

_____

_____

_____

_____

_____

_____

_____

_____

_____

_____

_____

_____

_____

_____

DO ONE THING EVERY DAY
THAT MAKES YOU
STAND OUT

_____   _____

_____   _____

_____   _____

_____   _____

_____   _____

_____   _____

_____   _____

_____   _____

_____   _____

○ Plan a meeting with a rad female CEO

○ Volunteer for a cause where you feel you can elicit real change

○ Have a chat with a woman author

○ Create a public awareness campaign

○ Support only women-run business for a month

○ Visit your local pride center

○ Research PFLAG chapters

○ Conduct a sit-in

○ Find volunteer opportunities that serve the underprivileged

○ Start an all-girl peer-to-peer education program

○ Post a social media broadcast about a community event

○ Tackle an issue that affects you

○ Start a peer-to-peer support group

○ Research women's rights in your state or community

○ Join an LGBTQ group

○ Look for ways to challenge stereotypes

○ Start a fundraising project

○ Research the ACLU organization

○ Help build coalitions that promote justice and understanding

○ Do one thing that supports women-centered careers

○ Design women power bumper stickers

○ Raise awareness of women-run organizations or businesses

THINGS I'VE DISCOVERED WHILE BEING *Fierce:*

1. _____

2. _____

3. _____

4. _____

5. _____

6. _____

7. _____

8. _____

9. _____

10. _____

11. _____

12. _____

13. _____

14. _____

15. _____

16. _____

17. _____

18. _____

19. _____

20. _____

21. _____

22. _____

23. _____

24. _____

25. _____

As you travel through the world, you're bound to have brilliant realizations, crazy insights and sudden inspiration—if you're open to them. Here's where you can write these things down.

RECORD YOUR AHA MOMENTS & DETERMINE HOW THEY WILL HELP YOU CONTINUE MOVING, ONLY FORWARD!

WELL EARNED *Rebel* BADGES

ALPHA *Female*

Raddest

WOMANIST

-THIS-
GIRL
CAN

Yes,
YOU
can

Girl
FREAKIN'
BOSS

Girl
POWER

CHAPTER SIX

....

DEFENDER

of Justice

DEFENDER
of Justice

....

This chapter serves the formidable, the
mighty ones, the impartial proponents,
the unyielding debaters and the heroic
defenders of all that is just.
Learn to show up in your world by seeking
to champion what's ethical and equitable,
being willing to see what's doubtlessly fair,
going to bat for justice and finding any
way to be the hero and defender for
all things right.

So, what's stopping you?!

Michelle Obama

"WHEN THEY GO LOW, WE GO HIGH."

....

BORN: January 17, 1964

Job: Former First Lady of the United States

FACT: Was a lawyer

FACT: Graduated from Harvard

FACT: Her nickname is "Miche" (pronounced "Meesh")

FACT: She skipped a year in school

FACT: She is the former associate dean at the University of Chicago

FACT: Her secret service code name was "Renaissance"

What's Michelle's championing story?

What might your championing story be?

_____

_____

_____

_____

_____

_____

_____

_____

_____

_____

_____

_____

_____

_____

_____

_____

_____

Two formidable judges
What makes them so ridiculously formidable?

. . . .

. . . .

_____

_____

_____

Two impartial mediators
What makes them so ridiculously impartial?

. . . .

. . . .

_____

_____

_____

Two powerful public speakers
What makes them so ridiculously powerful?

. . . .

. . . .

Two unyielding debaters
What makes them so ridiculously unyielding?

. . . .

. . . .

Two heroic human rights defenders
What makes them so ridiculously heroic?

. . . .

. . . .

DEVISE & CONQUER

(put something out into your world)

Come up with something *MIGHTY* to share with others (an event, a book, an idea, an experience, a film... Get creative, be clever, think unconventionally, use your imagination, develop a vision, take a giant leap, have an innovative mindset, do something mighty!) and then use a crowdfunding method to bring your small and mighty project to life!

PROJECT: _____

_____

_____

_____

_____

GOAL: _____

_____

_____

HOW YOU WILL GO ABOUT IT (PLAN, SCHEDULE, BUDGET):

_____   _____

_____   _____

_____   _____

WHY THIS PROJECT? (WHY IS IT IMPORTANT TO YOU AND WHY
IS IT IMPORTANT TO SHARE?):

_____

_____

_____

_____

_____

_____

_____

_____

Would you
RATHER?

(circle your answers)

SPEAK IN RHYMES *Or* HAVE TO SING EVERYTHING YOU SAY?

HAVE THE ABILITY TO READ OTHER PEOPLE'S MINDS *Or* THE ABILITY TO SEE INTO THE FUTURE?

GO THROUGH LIFE UNABLE TO ASK ANY QUESTIONS *Or* UNABLE TO ANSWER ANY QUESTIONS?

LIVE WITHOUT YOUR PHONE FOR TWO WEEKS *Or* YOUR COMPUTER FOR A MONTH?

SAVE YOUR COUNTRY FROM GOING TO WAR *Or* FROM A TERRIBLE DISEASE??

WIN A MILLION DOLLARS *Or* NEVER HAVE TO BUY ANYTHING FOR YOURSELF EVER AGAIN?

LET GO *Or* GET EVEN?

BE AVERAGE AT EVERYTHING *Or* AN EXPERT ON A SINGLE SUBJECT?

SAVE YOUR COUNTRY FROM INVASION *Or* FROM A NATURAL DISASTER

GIVE BAD ADVICE *Or* TAKE BAD ADVICE?

HAVE A REWIND *Or* A PAUSE BUTTON YOU COULD USE AT ANY TIME?

PLAY A VILLAIN *Or* A HERO IN A MOVIE?

EAT A SMALL CAN OF CAT FOOD *Or* TWO ROTTEN TOMATOES?

NOT BE ALLOWED TO WASH YOUR HANDS *Or* YOUR HAIR FOR A MONTH?

SEE INTO THE FUTURE *Or* INTO THE PAST?

BE A POLICE OFFICER *Or* A FIREFIGHTER?

What questions might you ask a supreme court judge, a prominent lawyer or a great debater?

Write down six mighty questions and choose a hotshot to interview!

1

_____

_____

_____

_____

2

_____

_____

_____

_____

3

_____

_____

_____

_____

4

5

6

(Look, I get it. We don't all know the rich and the famous, but you can surely reach out to some heavy hitters, some superheroes! Some of these grand humans might be a family member or a teacher or a business owner that you already know. Just remember, confidence is rad, so put some of daring in your back pocket and go for it!)

Scrupulous SCAVENGER

• • • • • • • • • • • • •

Set out on a scavenger hunt!
Take pictures, collect things
& size up your findings!

☐ AN UNEXPECTED CLUE

Date: Location:

Description:
_____

☐ THE WORD "JUSTICE"

Date: Location:

Description:
_____

☐ A PHOTO OF YOU IN FRONT OF
YOUR LOCAL COURTHOUSE

Date: Location:

Description:
_____

☐ THE BUSINESS CARD OF A LAWYER

Date: Location:

Description:
_____

☐ THE ENTRANCE SIGN TO A PRISON

Date: Location:

Description:
_____

☐ A WARNING SIGN

Date: Location:

Description:
_____

☐ A LAW BOOK

Date: Location:

Description:
_____

☐ THE SCALES OF JUSTICE

Date: Location:

Description:
_____

☐ A FLYER FOR A LOCAL COLLEGE
OR UNIVERSITY DEBATE CLUB

Date: Location:

Description:
_____

☐ A POLICE CAR

Date: Location:

Description:
_____

Notes:
_____

If you were to write, create, design or start a podcast around the idea of
Judicial Activism, what specific issues would excite you the most?
Who would be your audience? How do you think your audience would benefit
from listening? Write a short podcast pitch that could convince someone of
this brilliant idea!

ROOM for DEBATE

Engage with your friends, peers and comrades in a fiery debate. Put your civic debater skills to good use and research a topic that interests you. Research both sides and then outline your argument. Plan a time to meet with your other qualified pals and let the games begin!

Here are just a few mighty topics to get you started:

BANNED BOOKS

FREE COLLEGE

RECREATIONAL MARIJUANA

ZOOS

GUN CONTROL

STANDARDIZED TESTS

ANIMAL TESTING

BOTTLED WATER BAN

VOTING MACHINES

BINGE-WATCHING

DAYLIGHT SAVING TIME

MINIMUM WAGE

Now, go for it and outline your debate:

_____

_____

_____

_____

_____

_____

_____

_____

_____

BRAVERY IS...

Everything that made me feel brave this week:

What does *justice* mean to you? How would you define it?
List 10 words you would use to describe justice:

DO ONE THING EVERY DAY
THAT IS

INFLUENTIAL

Why NOT?

- ◯ Plan a meeting with a judge
- ◯ Write letters to your legislators to advocate for specific local laws
- ◯ Attend a public hearing
- ◯ Join the debate team
- ◯ Advocate for legislation
- ◯ Conduct a survey about an issue and share the results
- ◯ Follow a lawyer around for a day
- ◯ Make a visit to the court house
- ◯ Petition elected officials
- ◯ Find local ways to support public safety projects
- ◯ Research the Appleseed Network
- ◯ Find volunteer opportunities that serve lawbreakers
- ◯ Do one thing that supports local lawmakers
- ◯ Write a letter to a company you feel has done something unfair
- ◯ Take a lead role in a public protest
- ◯ Read a book about a supreme court justice
- ◯ Research the NAACP civil rights organization
- ◯ Research the prison-industrial complex
- ◯ Meet face-to-face with an elected official
- ◯ Raise money to contribute to addressing injustice
- ◯ Create a public awareness campaign
- ◯ Join a debate group
- ◯ Research crazy laws still on the books in your town
- ◯ Organize a protest on a law you oppose
- ◯ Be a whistle-blower

Volunteer, VOLUNTEER

Find a **judicial cause** to commit your time to! Volunteering your time can make all the difference for so many rad purposes in your community and world. Start by listing as many opportunities as you can think of or look up. Decide on one that interests you the very most and write down reasons why you'd be a good fit and how you feel you would make a difference. Then, go get 'em!

○ United We Dream

○ Planned Parenthood

○ American Civil Liberties Union

○

○

○

○

○

○

○

○

○

○

○

○

○

○

○

○

○

○

○

○

REASONS WHY:

WHAT  if?

Here's your chance to rewrite history.

Yes, for real! Well, on paper at least! What if there were no such thing as horses? Or, what if humans had never evolved the ability to digest meat? Or, what if the U.S. hadn't used nuclear attacks in World War II? Take the next few pages to make one of these stories yours. Pick a piece of history and revise it, rewrite it, amend the terrible bits, give it a little bit of an upgrade, make a new draft, revamp it and reexamine what you already know. Write things down!

Interesting scenarios to get your brain working:

What if John F. Kennedy survived the assassination attempt?

What if everybody in the world had the same skin tone?

What if Hitler had decided not to invade Russia?

What if the Confederate States won the American Civil War?

What if the Spanish flu epidemic in 1918 had killed 50% of the world's population?

What if Australia had been discovered and colonized by the Japanese?

What if the British Empire had invaded and conquered China?

What if there was no oil in the Middle East?

What if there were no such thing as horses?

What if all humans never evolved the ability to digest meat?

1. _____

2. _____

3. _____

4. _____

5. _____

6. _____

7. _____

8. _____

9. _____

10. _____

11. _____

12. _____

13. _____

14. _____

15. _____
_____
16. _____
_____
17. _____
_____
18. _____
_____
19. _____
_____
20. _____
_____
21. _____
_____
22. _____
_____
23. _____
_____
24. _____
_____
25. _____
_____
_____
_____
_____
_____
_____
_____
_____

Aha!

As you travel through the world, you're bound to have brilliant realizations, crazy insights and sudden inspiration—if you're open to them. Here's where you can write these things down.

RECORD YOUR AHA MOMENTS & DETERMINE HOW THEY WILL HELP YOU CONTINUE MOVING, ONLY FORWARD!

★ NOPE ★

Killing it

SUPER
GIRL

★
ROCKSTAR

GRL/PWR

GOLD
ST★R

GAME
changer

EPILOGUE

DECIDE 50 THINGS

YOU WANT TO DO THIS YEAR:

THINGS *to* REMEMBER

SIGNIFICANT QUOTES, KIND COMPLIMENTS, WORDS OF WISDOM:

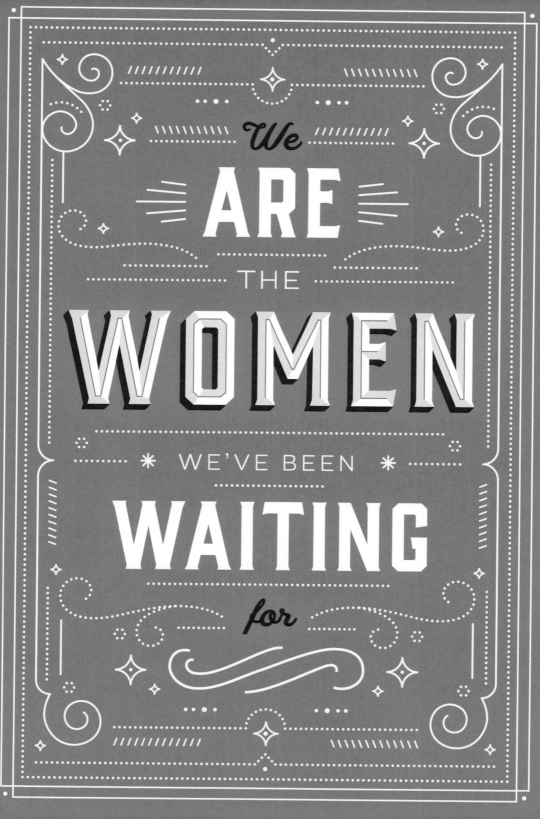

FIELD NOTES

JOTTINGS & MUSINGS

FIELD NOTES

JOTTINGS & MUSINGS